Information Security

Information Security
A Practical Handbook on
Business Counterintelligence

by

Henry W. Prunckun

Bibliologica Press

Information Security:
A Practical Handbook on Business Counterintelligence

ISBN 978-0-6485093-5-6

NATIONAL
LIBRARY
OF AUSTRALIA

A catalogue record for this
work is available from the
National Library of Australia

Originally published in 1989 by
Charles C. Thomas—Publisher,
Springfield, Illinois, USA

Web: bibliologica.com

Reprinted in 2020 by
Bibliologica Press
P.O. Box 656
Unley, South Australia, 5061
Australia

To my father, who, along time ago, taught me that whatever you wanted to know could be found in books.

PREFACE

This is a handbook on information security for businesses. It addresses a subject which I consider to be inadequately covered in the current body of security literature. I believe that apart from a limited number of Department of Defense manuals available to the public on the subject, comprehensive guidelines for the control of business information is grossly lacking.

This book's main intent is to acquaint the reader with the basics of information security. It attempts to do this by looking at what is best described as business intelligence. It is considered that by becoming familiar with the function, structure, and operational methods involved in business intelligence, the reader can establish, and confidently maintain, a high level of information security (business counterintelligence), thus minimising the threat posed by business adversaries.

My awareness that the business community lacked such advice was borne through personal experiences as a professional information gatherer. As an Investigator with the South Australian State Government, I was able to penetrate numerous businesses in order to legally obtain information to support either criminal charges or to provide senior public servants with "intelligence briefings" on their fraudulent commercial activities. Had the counter-measures which I outline in this text been practised by those businesses, I would not have been as successful as I was. I, therefore, considered that if a business, which does not want its affairs to be discovered (as in the case of criminal activity), can be so easily penetrated, what chances do legitimate businesses (which historically take even fewer security precautions) stand against an attack by a professional "spy-for-hire," a well organised criminal group, or even more threatening, a foreign government's intelligence service. This handbook was written, therefore, to provide vital, no-nonsense assistance to businesses in need.

This handbook is rather short as security books go. However, its brevity is intentional. I recognise that for the most part, managers and administrators do not have the free time required to read and digest large masses of information, no matter how important it may be. To achieve effective utilisation by the reader, I have divided the book into four chapters, each addressing a particular aspect of the information continuum. The first presents the reader with an examination of the structure of intelligence. This presentation gives the reader an overview of what is generally referred to as intelligence work. Basically, this chapter addresses the question of "who does it" in the intelligence industry. The chapter tries to show that the pursuit of a particular piece of information may not always be limited to the sights of one interest group. Often, confidential business information can be sought by, for instances, both a business adversary and a foreign government (friend and foe alike).

Chapter Two builds on the structure of intelligence organisations and agencies by depicting the functional categories within business intelligence. It allows the reader to put into perspective the various relationships which exist within the intelligence industry, in particular, business intelligence; relationships that the reader might not have been previously aware of or believed only existed in fiction. In this way, the reader can gain an appreciation of how information security fits into the total intelligence concept.

The third chapter describes several methods used by agents of business intelligence in information gathering. Both overt and covert sources of information are discussed, with attention being drawn specifically to audio surveillance devices, physical surveillance, and open and semi-open sources of documents. The topic was purposefully limited to these issues because it is considered that, although there may be many more methods of gathering information, none are more effective or as widely used by the professional espionage agent.

Chapter Four is the "piece de resistance." It is a concise and straightforward blueprint for business managers and administrators on information security. It can be used to provide guidance without any other reading of the text, or it can be read consecutively, following the theoretical framework described above.

Finally, there is a detailed contents page for fast reference. Several appendices are also supplied which contain security advise complimentary to that provided in the text.

I am grateful to several people for their assistance and support in writing this book. I would like to take the opportunity to thank Ann for checking the final manuscript and for the countless other things she did, which assisted in its publication. And to Orren for his patience in allowing me the time to research and write the text. I would also like to express gratitude to my former colleagues in the Criminal Investigation Section of the South Australian Department of Public & Consumer Affairs, namely David, Karl, Ray and Rod, for their expertise in investigation and intelligence work, over the years, proved to be my best teacher.

H. W. Prunckun
Australia

AUTHOR'S NOTE

In the interest of smooth reading, all references in this book to the male gender have been made for convenience only. The pronoun "he" shall be regarded as including both males and females.

CONTENTS

Information Security

CHAPTER ONE

STRUCTURE OF INTELLIGENCE

Intelligence is structured around four central types. Although each type of intelligence has a unique purpose, they are in many ways related. Importantly, the same methods of operation, tactics, devices, information storage systems and methods of analysis are used by each. In addition, information itself holds no bounds as to its usefulness, and a particular piece of information could conceivably be the target for more than one type of intelligence user. In other words, the primary difference between the various types of intelligence lies in their end purpose or broad general intent.

For the purpose of this handbook, the four major types of intelligence will be labelled as Foreign Policy, Law Enforcement, Business and Private. Technically, there is a fifth type of intelligence, namely Military Intelligence; however, in its treatment here, military intelligence will be combined with foreign policy intelligence because of its intimate alignment.

Foreign Policy Intelligence
Foreign policy intelligence is conducted by the various branches of a nation's armed forces, foreign diplomatic service and, depending on the country, its atomic energy authority. Western nations generally tend to have a central agency which acts to coordinate the numerous intelligence functions (see Chapter Two), agencies, and the collection and processing of information

from all sources. Eastern Bloc nations, in contrast, lean towards a unified system with one supreme agency taking on all three roles—collection, analysis and coordination.

The types of information sought by foreign policy intelligence analysts can be anything from the current political issues facing a foreign government, the health, education and social structures of the country, its social problems, and its legal institutions. They may include issues concerning the availability of world resources, international trade relationships and the state of the global monetary order. Without a doubt, they also seek information on foreign technological developments, nuclear matters and almost anything to do with foreign defence industries.

Business Intelligence
Business intelligence is concerned primarily with the acquisition of trade secrets and confidential commercial information from competing firms. This activity can occur on a local, regional, national, or even international basis.

Business intelligence is not only limited to the realms of corporations and businesses themselves but can also include private investigation firms, who specialise in this area (see Private Intelligence below) and the intelligence units of foreign nations.

Law Enforcement Intelligence
Law enforcement intelligence encompasses those agencies engaged in a counterintelligence function (see Chapter Two). They would include a nation's police and other law enforcement and regulatory agencies (these can be quite numerous), immigration and customs services and, as the case may be, a specific agency created to combat the threat from foreign and internal subversion, espionage, sabotage or terrorism.

Private Intelligence

The structure of private intelligence is very diverse, but for the purpose of this book, it will be limited to those firms and private agents, who offer their services and expertise in intelligence work to the general public for fee or reward. Although the term general public implies an individual, it will again be apparent that there is some overlap in what constitutes private intelligence and what may be business intelligence or even foreign policy intelligence. The final determination will ultimately depend on who does the hiring of the agent or researcher.

Private intelligence practitioners offer a range of specialist services that go beyond the bounds of the average private investigator or detective. Often, the private intelligence practitioner comes from a background in law enforcement, military or foreign policy intelligence work. Their specialties may be in background investigations or surveillance. They may have extensive training in the use of state-of-the-art optical or electronic audio surveillance equipment, and they would be familiar with the techniques of intelligence analysis. They may offer advice on business counterintelligence and electronic audio counter-measures (de-bugging). They may also specialise in personal security requirements for VIPs.

Private intelligence agencies, for the purpose of this definition, would also include those privately run organisations that maintain massive databases for specialised inquiry work, for example, credit reporting agencies.

CHAPTER TWO

FUNDAMENTALS OF BUSINESS INTELLIGENCE

CATEGORIES OF INTELLIGENCE

The term intelligence has two basic meanings—the first refers to a body of knowledge and the second to actions or processes employed to produce knowledge. Intelligence as a body of knowledge deals with an adversary, a potential adversary, or a possible area of operation that is useful to business leaders in planning and carrying out their objectives. As a process, intelligence is organised or categorised by its different functions. As such, an examination of the scope of intelligence is required so that business counterintelligence can be seen in its setting as part of the whole intelligence mosaic. This chapter deals with the fundamentals of intelligence and addresses the various functional categories found in intelligence work, in both meanings of the term.

Pure Intelligence Function and the Intelligence Process

The majority of intelligence related work within the business sphere falls into this category. Pure intelligence in this sense is the final outcome of processing raw information which has been collected from all sources—be it open, semi-open, official or covert in nature. Once the information is in the hands of a research or intelligence analyst, it is evaluated and any irrelevant information is discarded. The pieces of information relevant to the case under consideration are then analysed, interpreted, and formed into a finished "product." This product is then disseminated to the end user. Therefore, the intelligence process can be summarised as the production of meaningful, timely information on business matters after careful analysis.

In more detail, intelligence is created in a process consisting of a four step cycle, that is:

(a) the establishment of a plan for information collection;

(b) data collection;

(c) analysis and interpretation the information which was obtained; and

(d) the dissemination and utilisation of the resulting intelligence product in order to achieve the set objective(s).

As long as a specific operation is being conducted, the intelligence process will be continuously forming a cycle. As new information is being collected, other data will be stored and analysed. The resulting outcomes will be disseminated for either immediate use, and/or used to set new collection objectives.

The presentation of the intelligence "product" can take a variety of forms. It could be a background history on a company or one of its executives, a diagram of a company's office lay-out, identification of new projects being researched, a prediction about the intended release date of a new product, staff salaries, the classification and number of personnel on a company's payroll, and so on. These outcomes have two emphases: tactical and strategic. Tactical intelligence is information which contributes directly to the achievement of an immediate goal, whereas strategic intelligence relates to long term forecasts or broader conclusions on larger objectives. Although there appears to be a clear demarcation between these types of intelligence, in certain situations, a given piece of information may be relevant to both tactical objectives and strategic goals.

Counterintelligence Function

Counterintelligence is concerned with neutralising or destroying the effectiveness of an adversary's intelligence activities. Essentially, it is a security function. The thrust of counterintelligence is specifically to protect a business from infiltration by an adversary, to protect against inadvertent leakage of confidential information, and to make secure its installations and material against theft and sabotage.

As with tactical and strategic intelligence, there is also a thin line dividing pure intelligence and counterintelligence. That is, information concerning the opposition's attempts to penetrate one's business can feed into the intelligence cycle, revealing an opponent's information voids as well as his capabilities and possible intentions. It is to the issue of counterintelligence that Chapter Four is devoted.

Espionage Function

This is the classic form of information gathering dating back many centuries. It often forms part of the second and most important step of the intelligence cycle. Espionage, or spying, traditionally utilises undercover agents who are placed in positions which allow them to view, overhear or otherwise obtain confidential information.

With improvements in technology, however, there has been an ever-increasing swing away from the classic use of espionage and an accelerated move toward more technical means of espionage. The primary areas of development have been audio surveillance devices and special photographic equipment. The use of such tools can provide the intelligence analyst or researcher with an exponential gain in both the quantity and quality of the information gathered. Because of this development in intelligence work, Chapter Three explores the current state-of-the-art audio surveillance devices and optical and photographic surveillance equipment that may be used against a business.

Counterespionage Function

On the surface, counterespionage presents as being simple spying. It is somewhat related to counterintelligence but is an extremely precise function. It is the most subtle and sophisticated of all of the intelligence functions. It calls for the engineering of complex strategies that deliberately put one's agent(s) in contact with the opposition's intelligence personnel. This is done so that an adversary can be fed with "disinformation" which in turn will hopefully lead to confusion, thus disrupt their organisation and allowing the perpetrator to prosper.

Counterespionage has been described as the material of which spy novels are made. Counterespionage involves ingenious entrapments, agent provocateurs, counter-spies and double crosses (also see the section on Infiltration—Indirect, in Chapter Four).

Covert Action Function

Sometimes referred to as covert political action, this function lies in somewhat of a grey area of intelligence work. It uses the traditional methods of information gathering and analysis but also ties in such areas as advice and counsel, financial and material support, as well as technical assistance to individuals, groups or businesses who are opposed to or working in competition with, a target business.

Covert action is a function by which a business uses the information it collects to prop up and strengthen its allies and weaken, or ultimately destroy, its opponent(s). The effectiveness of covert action is contingent upon the perpetrator's involvement remaining hidden, or at the very least, deniable. If a "plausible denial" can be maintained, then the rewards of such ventures can be enormous. If, on the other hand, the perpetrator's involvement is discovered, the consequences of this activity can be catastrophic (e.g., the French Government's sabotage of the Greenpeace boat, Rainbow Warrior, in New Zealand on July 10, 1985).

CHAPTER THREE

INFORMATION GATHERING

OVERT SOURCES OF INFORMATION

Open and Semi-Open Sources

B ecause we live in an age were information is vital to every aspect of life, an astonishing variety of recorded information, for both public viewings and for commercial use, has evolved. It is because of these record systems that businesses, as well as individuals, generate what has become known as a "paper trail."

A paper trail can best be described as all records and documents created by an individual or business in the normal course of commercial and social interaction with other individuals, organisations, government departments and businesses (both public and private). These records and documents in effect leave a trail detailing where the individual (or business) has been, with whom he has had dealings, what goods and services he has purchased, what he owns, what his likes and dislikes are, and more importantly, what his intentions may be. To the agent, this trail forms a composite picture of the individual or business under surveillance. Uncovering one part of the paper trail can lead the agent to other sources of information. These sources are not only limited to those on "paper," but can be extended to interviews with people such as

11

friends, neighbors, and colleagues, perhaps using a pretext, and to physical and optical surveillance.

To the professional espionage agent, a paper trail can provide very valuable information indeed. It is the professional agent who will be ferreting out information with the intent of compromising either an executive or a business's viability in the marketplace. Law enforcement agencies collect similar raw information on criminals and organised crime groups. The value of this information in a collated and analysed form can be seen in the reported arrests of influential gang members, hitherto untouchable by the Law. This is particularly so in the United States.

Specific sources of open and semi-open information are limited only by the agent's imagination. Examples include, but are by no means limited to telephone directories (both current and back-dated); city directories; motor vehicle bureaus; vehicle license plates; drivers' licenses; birth, death and marriage records; civil and criminal court records; property titles, mortgage documents, liens and caveats; school records; voter registration lists; credit reporting agencies; utility companies; credit card companies; insurance companies; stockbrokers; moving companies; chambers of commerce; racing or gaming commissions; banks and finance companies; the Post Office; various government departments, agencies and statutory authorities (local, state and national—these can be almost limitless!); employment agencies; and public and university libraries. In addition to an almost infinite amount of information contained in library stacks, libraries have reference books of every description, maps, newspapers, journals, periodicals, registers, and catalogues. There are also private "special libraries," including private computer databanks, that contain topics of particular interest. The United States has its Government Printer, Library of Congress, Congressional Record, The National Archives, United Nations Publications, its oral history collections, and information available through the Freedom of Information Act. In other countries there exist equivalents. Finally, there are public radio and television broadcasts which have the potential of providing an extremely wide range of information, as do photographic and motion picture archives.

COVERT SOURCES OF INFORMATION

Physical Surveillance

Physical surveillance is the making of visual observations of people, vehicles, or activities at various locations. Physical surveillance may take place either at a fixed location, which is known as a "stake-out," or in a continually moving situation, referred to as a "tail." Physical surveillance is often used to supplement information which has been obtained from open or semi-open sources. It can also be used early in an operation to accelerate the generation of leads, corroborate existing information, or to simply obtain details that normally would not be available through other avenues of inquiry.

Optical Surveillance

Because professional agents rely so heavily on their eyesight in conducting physical surveillance, various devices are used to assist in extending their vision. Employing this technology also assists an agent to position himself much further away from the subject than could normally be achieved with unaided sight, thus reducing the possibility of unwanted discovery.

The principle and traditional device used in physical surveillance is a pair of binoculars. Binoculars are an optical device consisting of two prism-operated telescopes fixed in parallel. This configuration enables a surveillant to view a magnified image of the subject using both eyes. Binoculars have been designed to provide both magnifying power and light gathering capabilities. The latter is essential for surveillance work at dusk and at night.

Viewing a subject at distances which exceeds the effective range of binoculars is accomplished by using another traditional device—a telescope. The magnifying power of the telescope ranges from twenty to several hundred times that of normal vision. Binoculars on the other hand range from about six to twenty times that of normal vision.

A viewing device usually at home in submarines, but which is frequently used in land-based information gathering, is the periscope. Small portable high-quality devices are used to peer into high, inaccessible windows, over walls and around corners. Periscopes are also used in applications such as surveillance vans.

Recent developments in optical technology have given birth to several new low light (night) viewers. These units are designated as either "active" or "passive" night vision devices. The first group, the active devices, operate by using an infrared light beam. The surveillant projects the invisible beam of energy so that it illuminates the subject. The image is then viewed with special equipment which converts the infrared radiation into the visible light spectrum. The second range of devices operate by amplifying the existing background light - moon, stars, streetlights and so on—by several thousand times, thus literally turning night into day through the sights of the surveillant's night scope.

Covert Photography

By far, the most commonly used camera in covert photography is the thirty-five-millimetre, single lens, reflex (SLR). However, in some unique situations, such as surreptitious copying of documents, a subminiature camera would usually be employed. Obviously, the value of subminiature cameras in the latter case lies in their concealable size. The advantages of thirty-five-millimetre SLR's are, on the other hand, their "fast" (light sensitive) lenses, and the universal availability of a wide variety of film types.

Under low light conditions or at night, the normal range of photographic films can be by-passed by for the newer, ultra-high speed and infrared sensitive films. These film stocks are specifically designed for the most trying lighting conditions. They ensure that the surveillant obtains the highest possible number of successful image recordings. In addition, fast films and lenses can be assisted in producing quality low light photographs by a special film processing technique that in effect, boosts the film's light sensitivity. This technique is known as push-processing.

As with binoculars and telescopes in physical observation, telephoto lens play an important role in covert photography. Reflective mirror (catadioptric) lenses not only enable a surveillant to greatly reduce the physical size of his equipment, making concealment easier; they act to extend the agent's operational distances. Basically, catadioptric lenses use a system of mirrors to compress the light's optical path. Magnification (measured in the focal length of the lens) varies from about one hundred to two thousand millimetres.

16mm and Super-8 motion picture cameras are also popular for surveillance work. These cameras are larger than SLRs, so they are often used with a telephoto lens, thus allowing the surveillant to record his observations from safe distances. In the case of fixed position surveillance (a stake-out), a "time lapse" option can be used to provide up to 48 hours of coverage from a 50 ft roll of film. In order to achieve this, time lapse photography operates in a single frame mode at greatly reduced speeds.

Aerial Photography
Aerial photography from both rotary and fixed wing aircraft is another effective method of information gathering. The history

of aerial surveillance dates to the mid-19th century when the first photograph was taken from a French military (hot air) balloon.

Since that time, many major developments have occurred in photo-reconnaissance. The technology currently available ranges from secret reconnaissance satellites and ultra-sophisticated spy planes down to the light plane or helicopter with conventional hand-held photographic equipment. The former of course are used by intelligence agencies of various nations, while the latter would probably be used on a rental basis by a private detective, spy-for-hire, or investigative journalist.

Video Recording Systems

With the advent of compact and hand-held video cameras and fibre optic lens, optical surveillance has moved into new areas of use, greatly expanding on photography's traditional applications. For instance, the professional espionage agent currently has access to video cameras built into such items as briefcases, books, wall clocks, paintings, and even into plants that appear to decorate an executive's office.

Electronic Surveillance

The use of electronic devices in surveillance has become a pervasive and permanent phenomenon in today's society. The rapid advance in the state-of-the-art of electronics and the open accessibility of this technology has placed these devices within reach of any interested party. For example, kits and instructions are readily available from most electronic shops, and for less than $75 worth of electronic components, a very sophisticated bug, wiretap or other listening device can be constructed. These electronic intruders, therefore, put every business at great potential risk.

The fundamental principle of any audio surveillance operation is to be able to plant a quality microphone as near as possible to the person(s) under surveillance and, in doing so,

16

avoid background noise that may render the intercept useless. The types of microphones used in audio surveillance are required by the nature of the work to be very small and are referred to in the trade as "sub-miniature." Their minute size allows them to be secretly deployed in the environment under surveillance. Once in place , they can be connected to a high gain amplifier, and then either to headphones (for "live" monitoring), a tape-recorder (for listening at a later time), or a transmitter (to reduce the chance of detection by broadcasting the conversation to a distance listening station).

If a transmitter is not used in an operation, the wires leading from the microphone to the listening/amplifying equipment must be concealed to prevent its detection. In some cases, existing wires such as telephone, electrical or even paradoxically, burglar alarm wires, can be used instead of running new wires, thus making detection more difficult. There are also special metal paints on the market which an agent can use to "paint" wires across a room. Once touched-up with paint of the surrounding decor, these "wires" are reported to be very difficult to detect.

There are several types of microphones the professional agent can use depending on the situation. They are the tube, contact/spike, pneumatic and directional microphones.

Tube microphones are designed to be inserted into a targeted room via a very small drill hole. This specie of microphone consists of an element connected to a thin tube. The tube emerges flush with the wall in the targeted room and practically, can only be detected by very close inspection. Tube microphones are likely to be located in spots made classic in spy novels—behind a wall, a picture, a piece of furniture, that is anything that would hinder detection for as long as possible.

Contact and spike microphones, in contrast, require less effort to secure their installation. These microphones do not respond to air vibration as a conventional microphone does, but rather translates vibration into sound. Contact microphones are like the "pick-ups" used by musicians to amplify their instruments and spike microphones resemble the phonograph needle. These types of microphones are simply attached to the exterior of a wall, window, floor, or ceiling. Once in place, these devices will reproduce quite clearly the sounds produced within the targeted room. These microphones lend themselves ideally to permanent installation.

The pneumatic cavity microphone is the electronic version of the glass tumbler against the wall trick, historically recognized as an effective method for monitoring adjacent room conversations. This type of microphone is substantially superior, however, and operates by using a specially constructed shell which is highly responsive to surface vibrations at audio frequencies found in the range of human speech. This "cavity" is used in conjunction with a conventional microphone element to enhance the microphone's performance. It also forces audio output to correspond to a wall's surface (or window, floor or ceiling depending on the case) vibrations rather than a direct sound output.

Directional microphones are of two types: parabolic and shotgun. Parabolic microphones consist of a "dish" with an inwardly pointing microphone element. The targeted audio is reflected and focused on the microphone element, thus gaining a directional effect. The shotgun (also known as a rifle or machine gun) microphone operates on the same principle, but utilizes a long tube, or set of tubes, in a cluster to home in on the targeted conversation. The effective range of these microphones is reported to be about 160 meters, and they are known to be able to pick up audio through closed windows at closer distances.

Another area of audio surveillance discussed briefly above, is that of wireless microphones, also known as miniature transmitters. These devices rank further up the hierarchy in surveillance sophistication. Transmitters offer an agent much greater safety from detection because installation is virtually effortless. These devices do not have any wires or connections to reveal their location. They can be attached to furniture or fixtures by means of a magnet or adhesive surface, or concealed in everyday objects such as rings, pens, cigarette lighters, books, ashtrays or pictures. Transmitters do not require the eavesdropper, or his equipment, to be located nearby. Their range of transmission varies from sixty meters to one kilometre. It is directly dependent upon transmitter strength, the thickness of surrounding walls, the sensitivity of the receiver and, to a smaller extent, on the weather.

Body transmitters are generally larger, more powerful and better constructed than wireless microphones. This is because the chance of detection is slight, and the device is intended to be used repeatedly. These devices are designed to operate from an agent's coat pocket, under-clothing, or attached by tape directly to the agent's body.

Akin to the body transmitter is the briefcase transmitter. Not only can this device be used by a "walk-in spy," but it can be conveniently "forgotten" in an office of a business's in order to obtain the ensuing conversations. (see also the use of briefcase video cameras—Covert Photography)

Another type of electronic surveillance transmitter operates by broadcasting in the very low frequency (VLF) range. This device uses electrical power lines for signal transmission. The signals move along the wire path and, because of the device's very low frequency, very little energy is radiated into space. This method of communication is used by many of the "wireless intercoms" sold commercially.

Communication equipment which operates outside of the standard radio broadcast frequencies tends to be more secure from interception. This is because the radio receivers needed for reception are difficult to obtain. These radio receivers are the microwave devices used by telephone companies for telecommunications and by private enterprises for computer data transmission. Such receivers are complicated in design and very expensive, although military and governmental intelligence agencies would have ready access to these. Units used for intercepting microwave communications can be set up in a van or building anywhere along the path between the transmitter and the receiver, which could be several hundred miles.

Several devices, although not specifically designed for surveillance work, are worthy of a brief note because their function provides the professional espionage agent with an increased scope of application. These are the drop-out relay, the voice-operated-relay (VOX), and the carrier switch.

The drop-out relay is attached to the target's telephone line and then wired to a transmitter. It will switch the bug on whenever the hand-piece is lifted from its cradle and off when it is replaced. This prolongs battery life, and because the bug is not transmitting continuously, it lowers the risk of being detected by an electronic counter-measures sweep. (see Chapter Four—Audio Surveillance for more on electronic countermeasures)

A VOX is similar in purpose to the drop-out relay. If connected to a room transmitter, the bug remains dormant until activated by the sound of a voice or noise. The VOX turns the bug on and off as individuals enter and leave the targeted room.

Finally, a carrier switch can be used to start and stop a tape recorder when it receives an audio signal, and it can be activated by a hidden transmitter. Employed in conjunction with a drop-out relay or a VOX, the switch carrier increases exponentially the surveillance capabilities of the agent.

The telephone is another medium of electronic surveillance. Audio "penetrations" involve two methods. The first method uses devices which intercept conversation directly from telephone lines and requires no entry into the target's premises. The second method is one which uses a portion of the telephone system for room eavesdropping and usually requires physical entry into the premises. (see also the section on Placement of Audio Surveillance Devices in Chapter Four)

Because the telephone company provides all the electrical power required to operate a subscriber's telephone service, this medium offers great eavesdropping benefits to the professional agent. For example, the telephone's power supply can be used to directly operate electronic eavesdropping devices, the wires themselves can be used to carry the resulting audio signals, and the microphone in the handset can be used to listen in on room conversations.

The techniques used to tap conversation from telephone lines consist of (a) direct wire connections, and (b) induction coils. In direct wire connections, the lines are cut, and the listening device spliced in place, using an electronic matching network. With induction coils, the tapping process literally lifts the audio signals off the telephone line and therefore does not require splicing. For this reason, induction coils can prove to be undetectable by electronic counter-measure sweeps. The only effective way to detect this type of bug is by visual inspection of the telephone wiring.

An alternative to direct wire connections is a radio system. This is the same as the wireless microphones described previously, except that it requires no microphone element. This is because the audio signals are already in an electrical form. Radio systems use the telephone line voltage for power, as opposed to batteries, and transmit whatever conversations are on the targeted line to a remote receiver/tape recorder.

The placement of telephone surveillance devices can be quite arbitrary; the only limit to their deployment would be the ability of an agent to gain access to the target's telephone system.

The devices may be installed within the telephone instrument itself, anywhere along the line in the targeted building, on a telephone pole outside the building, or in the wiring closet or terminal room where the lines are joined to the branch feeder cable.

There are several other electronic telephone surveillance devices which allow an agent to record the telephone numbers and dates when dialled by a target but do not permit the recording of the conversation. These are the dial impulse recorder, commonly referred to as a pen register, and the touch tone decoder. They operate simply by counting the impulses in each dial pulse group, that is, the digit dialled. An alternative to these two devices is the variable speed tape recorder. This operates by recording the desired conversation, then replaying it at a reduced speed so that the impulses can be counted to determine the number dialled.

The harmonica bug, or infinity transmitter, is the principal eavesdropping device used for planting within the telephone instrument itself. This device is basically a tone-controlled switch, coupled with an audio amplifier and a microphone. Although it uses the telephone system, the device functions as a room eavesdropper as opposed to a telephone conversation interceptor. The infinity transmitter uses the existing telephone lines for conveying the surreptitiously acquired conversation. It is activated from an infinite distance by a tone generator similar to those used by answering machines. The tone is 440hz, a 'C' note on a harmonica, giving it its second name.

In order to operate the infinity transmitter, the agent dials the target telephone number, which can be local, interstate or international. After dialling the number, but before the telephone rings, a harmonica is blown, or a tone beeper is sounded into the agent's telephone mouthpiece. On the target telephone, the infinity transmitter receives the audio tone and switches the device to answer this telephone electrically rather than physically. If this is performed correctly, the target telephone should not ring. This, in effect, means that the telephone is working even though the hand piece remains on the cradle. Once operational, an agent may monitor the room conversation. If the subject attempts to use the telephone, the agent simply hangs up, and the device is electrically disconnected, returning the instrument to normal operation.

There are several other techniques directed at modifying the telephone instrument for eavesdropping. This form of electronic surveillance exploits the normal operation of the entire telephone system. By shorting or by-passing the hook-switch on the instrument it causes the telephone to become a live microphone. This technique is known as telephone "compromising."

Another dimension to electronic surveillance is the systems which operate using directional beams of light energy. These systems are based on the use of laser beams of either visible or infrared energy to convey their intercepted audio. They are reported to be quite reliable and virtually undetectable. The systems consist of a laser light source which focuses its beam on a window in a targeted room, and an optical receiving/decoding device. The system operates by detecting minute vibrations of the reflected beam caused by the room's audio. Decoding of these vibrations reproduces the conversation or sounds within.

Interception of computer data can be accomplished in similar ways to eavesdropping on room conversations. With data interception, the legitimate user's data transferral is intercepted through a suitable wiretap or bug, and either recorded or transmitted to a listening post as is done in the case of audio. With the interception of computer data, an agent monitors the data exchange from terminal to the main computer, thereby tabulating input data and computer responses.

CHAPTER FOUR

INFORMATION SECURITY

Initial Considerations

The recommendations outlined in this chapter are not intended to be rigid in their adaptation, but rather flexible in their approach. The reader must consider many factors before implementing the following counter-measures. Important considerations that affect the establishment (or up-grading) of a counterintelligence program include, but are by no means limited to, financial constraints and the willingness of staff to follow proposed procedures once enacted. There is little sense, for example, in spending large sums of money on an intruder detection system if it may push a budding business to the brink of insolvency. Likewise, staff may be tempted to by-pass security procedures if those procedures are viewed as overly complicated or time-consuming.

The counter-measures outlined here can be adapted either in whole or in part, depending on the circumstances of the business. The important fact is that the principles of counterintelligence are observed and that periodic inspections are carried out to check on the standard of security practised.

Identifying Levels of Threat

Threat identification is the initial step for any business when establishing a counterintelligence effort. Likewise, it becomes an ongoing consideration once an counterintelligence capability has been developed. Listed below are three major, or broad band, sources of threat. This list is intended to give the reader an appreciation of the hierarchy of threats that his business may face during normal trade. Steps taken to thwart intelligence collection at, for example, a Level 2 threat would be sufficient to guard against any attempt by the inferior Level 3 threat, but not the reverse. This is an important factor to remember. It is critical for businesses to determine where their threats lay before deciding on the range and depth of security measures they will require. Furthermore, a business's threat level may change from time to time due to the dynamics of its operations. Therefore, its security needs will also be required to either escalate or abate in response to these changing conditions.

Level 1 Threat. Surveillance by a foreign government's security or intelligence agency, or surveillance by one's own national law enforcement/intelligence organization(s).

Level 2 Threat. Surveillance by a state/local law enforcement or intelligence unit, an organized criminal group, a foreign, or domestic business competitor employing a "spy-for-hire," a private detective acting on behalf of a party interested in your business's affairs, or other professional fact finders (e.g., investigative journalist).

Level 3 Threat. Non-professional surveillance by, for example, an employee, a business associate/competitor, or another interested individual or group acting on their own for profit or revenge.

Classification of Information
In order to foil possible attempts by a professional espionage agent to penetrate a business, information about the business and its activities should be divided into classifications of sensitivity. Further, these classifications should be used as a guide when releasing or disseminating information. Information in this

context means knowledge which requires protection from disclosure include such areas as:

- production plans;
- production methods;
- production schedules;
- new product releases and intending dates;
- marketing strategies;
- new advertising campaigns;
- customer/client lists;
- trading terms and agreements;
- details of alliances with other firms;
- proposed mergers;
- policy directives;
- rationalization plans;
- sales projections;
- material costs;
- supply sources;
- tenders;
- research initiatives;
- technical discoveries;
- personnel (their numbers, positions, salary packages and expertise); and
- employee recruitment, promotions, transfers and dismissal details.

The lowest classification of information, designated as Grade 4, consists of information of a general and unrestricted nature. The type of information provided in company prospectuses is a good example of this. Such information would be suitable for all general inquiries.

The next highest classification, Grade 3, consists of information which should be available to clients only upon request. Information of this type is best described as information and/or material that, if disclosed to an adversary, could reasonably be expected to cause some degree of "damage" to the business.

Moving up the scale again is Grade 2 information. This information should be available to a business's largest and most important clients. Information with this designation would be information and/or material that, if disclosed inappropriately, could reasonably be expected to cause "serious damage" to a business.

Finally, the most sensitive information, Grade 1, should be available only to staff with a need-to-know and government departments which have appropriate authority. Information of this type, if disclosed to an adversary, would reasonably be expected to cause "exceptionally grave damage" to a business. Staff authorized to access documentation of this grade should be required to sign a "chain of custody record" in order to assure control over its content (see Appendix A). The chain of custody record also facilitates withdrawal and destruction when the documentation is no longer required (also see the section on Document Disposal).

To inform staff members of a particular document's degree of sensitivity, each document should be identified with a marking indicating its grade (rubber stamped 1-4 in red ink). When marking a document, it should be kept in mind that perhaps not all of the document needs to classified at a particular sensitivity level. Take, for example, a report compiled about a recent business operation. It is ideal for public release in a future marketing campaign (Grade 4), but a page (or even several paragraphs) contains technical data about the operation that is best kept reserved. That section can carry a Grade 2 stamp, while the remainder of the text displays the general Grade 4 classification.

By using an information classification system, inappropriate disclosure is less likely to occur, and as the information contained in various documents becomes dated and less sensitive with the passage of time, reclassifying the information's grade downwards can then take place. Obviously, the extent to which a business goes in enacting a classification system is determinate upon its size. Sole proprietors and professional consultants will need far fewer formal arrangements than larger businesses. Businesses of any size will have to adopt much more formal systems.

Accounting Practices

Although the previous section—Classification of Information— addressed the need to grade information by its level of sensitivity in the broad sense, it is worth discussing the accounting practices of businesses specifically. For, if accounting practices are not taken into consideration when classifying information, such loopholes can create serious weaknesses in a counterintelligence program.

Accounting is the practice of identifying, measuring and communicating economic information about a business. Arguably, it is one of the most valuable sources of information for planning and control a business has. Careful consideration should, therefore, be given to safeguarding financial data about sensitive matters. Such information should not be recorded openly in journals and the ledger along with supply items and petty cash purchases. Sensitive projects, whatever they may be, should have special accounting practices designed to minimize the risk of exposing their budgets, expenditures and the like to staff who preform only routine accounting tasks.

Advertisements

Advertisements and editorial articles appearing in the media are areas worthy of note. Such information can be very revealing about a business. All information contained in advertisements for personnel, prestige, product or service development, technical advancements or marketing should be analyzed as possible "intelligence" for use by a business competitor or agent. Even the size of an advertisement and the frequency at which it appears are in themselves important factors when analyzing a business's intentions and strategies. Likewise, the type of media a business uses and the positioning of an advertisement in the publication can also provide vital pieces of information. The same applies to editorial information. Clients are not the only readers of such media articles; a professional agent will be privy to them also. In order to combat unwitting disclosure, a review procedure should be set up to screen information intended for publication or presentation at public meetings. (see section Classification of Information)

Compromised Information

If sensitive information has been compromised or just "lost," the following guidelines will assist a business in minimizing the damage that may result:

(a) Attempt to regain custody of the documents/material.

(b) Assess the information which has been compromised (or subjected to compromise) to ascertain the potential damage and institute action necessary to minimize the effects of the damage.

(c) Investigate to establish the weakness in the security arrangements which caused or permitted the compromise and alter these arrangements to prevent any recurrence.

(d) Take appropriate action to educate/counsel/discipline the person(s) responsible if this can be established.

Audio Surveillance

For obvious reasons, it is impossible to determine the extent of electronic eavesdropping which exists in the business community, although from media reports it appears to be quite widespread and not limited to any one industry or commercial sector. If a business suspects it is the target of either an illegal wiretap or bug, an audio counter-measure sweep is the best way of determining if there are any listening devices in operation. The sweep, however, will reveal devices operating at that given time only. It must be stressed that no room can be guaranteed to be proof against audio surveillance. Even the most sensitive rooms in the United States Embassy in Moscow have been reported to have been penetrated. Conducting sweeps at non-constant intervals is, therefore, the most effective way of combating the threat of audio surveillance. It is the most reliable way known to check for, and clear, audio surveillance devices.

There are limitations however, to this type of service. Firstly, with regard to telephones, even if your business's telephone instrument(s) appears to be clear, there is no way of determining whether the telephone of another party is under surveillance by inspecting your end of the line. There is also no technology available to date which can check for listening devices at, or beyond, the central telephone exchange. Secondly, there are some state-of-the-art devices and techniques used by intelligence agencies, and possibly very well-financed competitors and criminal groups, which may be undetectable because of their high level of sophistication. (for a list of audio surveillance devices and a brief description of their application, see Appendix E)

Audio counter-measure sweeps are conducted by both specialist business counterintelligence firms and by private detectives and investigators. Such services are usually listed in the "Yellow Pages" of the local telephone directory. A professional sweep should include both a through physical search, inspecting literally every inch of, and every object in the suspected area, and an electronic sweep. The electronic sweep may utilize a broad-band receiver and/or a specially designed field-strength meter to test for transmitters. Metal detectors can be used to hunt for bugs in non-metallic objects and deeply planted devices in walls, floors, and ceilings. There are also a wide range of meters used to test the telephone line voltage for the presence of wire taps.

Placement of Surveillance Devices

If audio surveillance devices were to be placed in a business's offices, it would most likely be accomplished by one or more of the following time-proven espionage methods:

(a) "friendly" access;

(b) surreptitious entry;

(c) infiltration; or

(d) secreted in a "gift."

Friendly Access

Access to a business's offices should be limited to employees and visitors, who are known or have appointments. All other visitors should be carefully screened, and their identities verified prior to entry. People making deliveries, including mail deliveries and maintenance workers, should be handled in the same manner. Access to offices should be on a restricted, need-to-be-there basis. If a business's visitor/staff traffic is heavy, a system of custom designed identity cards worn on employees' outer clothing can be an efficient method of quickly establishing "friend" or "foe." Toilets and other isolated places should be checked at the end of the day's business for intruders hiding in the building.

Surreptitious Entry

Break-ins and burglaries are not an uncommon occurrence for businesses to experience. However, in June 1972, "Watergate" brought home the reality that break-ins are not only a method for acquiring cash and valuable physical assets, but they are also a technique for information gathering. In intelligence work, this technique is referred to as a "black bag operation." Surreptitious entries are used to plant surveillance devices or to carry out other covert intelligence gathering activities. Short of creating a mini fortress, there is nothing which will make an office 100%

burglar-proof—even Buckingham Palace has had its intruder. There are, however, several steps that can be taken, which will reduce the likelihood of penetration by a professional agent. These are as follows:

(a) **Windows.** All windows should be protected by a suitable locking device. Keyed window locks provide a high level of security because an intending intruder can cut or smash the glass to reach and open any non-keyed device. Keyed locks also prevent windows from being opened for use as an exit by a successful intruder. Other window security devices include bars and grills. These are a must for air vents, fan openings, and skylights.

Reflective window tinting is another excellent counter-measure. Although not intended to prevent entry, reflective tinting provides a high level of protection for staff, equipment and processes contained within. By denying a surveillant knowledge of what is inside a building, a business can increase its level of physical security. An alternative to window tinting is the use of translucent glass.

(b) **External doors.** External doors should be solidly constructed and have three hinges per door. The installation of an additional hinge contributes greatly to the door's resistance against forced entry. Hardwood doors are better than those constructed of softwood, and solid doors are stronger than ones containing panels. However, wood panelled doors are more secure than doors containing glazed panels.

It is equally important to have strong door frames to prevent failure during an attack. Door frames should be securely fixed to the wall by appropriate bolts. Furthermore, double cylinder deadlocks should be installed on all external doors. The double cylinder deadlock needs a key to open it from either inside or outside and when in use, it prevents an intruder from using the door as an exit after the intrusion. The deadlock system also offers a medium to high degree of protection against "picking." There are also multi-locking systems which incorporate vertical bolts and rods designed to reinforce the door in conjunction with the deadlock option.

(c) **Lighting.** A protective lighting system is essential for the hours of darkness, otherwise, precautions taken to fortify perimeter barriers are placed under increased risk of attack. A good lighting system should be designed to:

- provide sufficient illumination to deter entry and make detection certain;
- provide against the failure of a single light which might leave a dark area in the system;
- eliminate heavily shadowed areas; and
- be proof against intentional destruction.

(d) **Intruder detection systems.** Intruder alarms will not prevent the physical entry of a professional espionage agent; however, the installation of a system could add an exponential level of deterrence. It must be stressed that the concern here is not with the protection of tangible assets such as cash, precious metals, art works or other material goods which could easily be converted into cash, but rather with information protection. Protection of tangible assets may require an extensive alarm system.

By installing an intruder detection system, the intention is to achieve a level of security in line with the level of sensitivity of the information being protected, not absolute security. It should be kept in mind that a professional agent will gain a greater advantage by obtaining the targeted information without the business's knowledge. It is, therefore, less likely that entry into an area or document storage "container" protected by an alarm would be attempted as it would alert the business to the fact that sensitive information has been compromised. (see the section on Document Storage in this Chapter) On the other hand, it is possible that a professional agent could disguise such a penetration as a property burglary or even an act of vandalism, hoping to throw any subsequent investigation off the track.

It is also important to note that not all areas of a business's offices must have a high level of physical security to protect its sensitive documentary information. A particular office or meeting room can be designated as "the" area in which the most sensitive information is held, and other offices can retain lower level documents used routinely. In this case, only the "secure room" needs to be considered for an intruder alarm system.

This same principle applies to electronic eavesdropping. A particular office or meeting room can be reserved for confidential discussions. Likewise, only this room would need to be fitted with an intruder detection system (and possibly soundproof insulation). Alternatively, such a "secure room" could be used for both sensitive meetings and the storage of confidential documents.

(e) Key control. A system of key control is essential for the prevention of unauthorized persons obtaining or duplicating keys. All existing keys and their corresponding locks should be catalogued. Keys currently issued should be signed for, and they should be collected when a person terminates his employment. If a key is lost, the lock, or its cylinder, should be replaced. It is important not to label keys with their purpose; if necessary, use a color code.

(f) Illegal entry. If a business discovers that its offices have been broken into, the Police should be notified at once. It is important to remember not to disturb obvious evidence that may assist the Police in their investigations. The guidelines outlined in the section on Compromised Information above should then be followed.

Infiltration—Pretext, Ruse, Disguise

Another espionage technique used in penetrating businesses is that of infiltration. The pretext, ruse and disguise offer a professional agent a plausible, common-sense technique for obtaining confidential information from your business.

Basically, there are four types of infiltration:

(a)   By telephone.   This method is used by the professional espionage agent, usually on a one-time basis in order to obtain general information about a business. It is the safest and most innocuous type of infiltration to perpetrate. This type of infiltration is carried out by simply telephoning the target business, then using a "pretext," attempting to extract as much information as possible.   Several calls could be made to a business over a period.   On the surface, each call would appear to be unrelated, but each would be designed to obtain specific pieces of information.   Depending on the pretext and the number of pretext calls made, the depth of information a professional agent could gather would (should!) probably be restricted to Grade 4 information.   It is therefore prudent to consider calls from unknown persons as potential infiltrations and to be conscious of the depth of information furnished.

It is important to beware of telephone pollsters. They may well be making a pretext call. If in doubt the identity of a telephone caller can sometimes be confirmed by requesting the caller's telephone number. The number can then be verified by using the telephone directory or with Directory Assistance before calling the party back (known as confirmation by "call-back").

(b)   By mail.   This is another low-grade form of infiltration.   Again, using a pretext, a professional espionage agent will write to a target business requesting information. The warning signs of a mail infiltration are the use of post office boxes, business name "fronts" and interstate addresses.

(c) In person. Direct personal infiltration of a business by a professional agent may follow pretext contacts by telephone and mail infiltration, and physical surveillance (see Countering

Physical Surveillance below). In this way, an agent can gather enough information to establish a "cover" for direct penetration or acquaint himself with the information needed for recruiting a proxy to carry out the task. The latter may even involve bribery and black-mail.

(d) Indirectly. This infiltration technique is complex to organize and run but can yield impressive results. Basically, a professional espionage agent creates a covert "business" or "organization" designed to draw a targeted business, or a member of its staff, to it. The bogus business is totally controlled by the agent. The agent's covert "organization" can be as simple as a trade newsletter or as elaborate as a fully operational business. Once established, the agent uses this front to extract and gather information which will assist his sponsor's business and/or subvert yours (see the section on Counterespionage Function in Chapter Two).

An example of this is the advertising of positions in a "new" and very attractive sounding business. The business may offer a salary and fringe benefit package more than those offered in the current market to entice targeted professionals or tradespeople. Once curriculum vitaes are received, they are analyzed for the desired information. If they do not disclose the information which is sought, additional information will be requested from the applicant and/or a personal interview conducted. The agent, or someone from his bogus organization, would then pump the vulnerable applicant for information about his present employer.

Gifts

Businesses should very carefully examine all gifts received anonymously for signs of concealed eavesdropping devices. There have been numerous cases were gifts have housed listening devices. Most notable was the 1952 presentation of The Great Seal of the United States to the American Embassy in

Moscow by the Russian government. The gift contained a very sophisticated bug. A prudent practice would be to inspect all office gifts, even if they originate from "friendly" sources.

Telephone Wiring

Wiretapping is the interception of telephone, telex and facsimile communication and computer data which is transmitted over telephone lines. As previously discussed in the sections on Audio Surveillance (Chapter Four) and Electronic Surveillance (Chapter Three), the interception of these signals can take place anywhere between the sender's offices and those of the receiver. The most vulnerable parts of the telephone system are the office's telephones and other data transmitting equipment, and the lines leading out of the building. Once the targeted line(s) leaves the building, interception is more difficult, but certainly not impossible. Apart from a counter-measure sweep, the chief counter-measure against wiretapping is to ensure that the telephone wiring closet, or terminal box, is equipped with a substantial locking device and that it remains secure at all times. In addition, all exposed wiring, or wiring that is easily accessible, should be shielded in conduit.

Cordless and Mobile Telephone

Although cordless telephones offer many advantages over their wire-bound cousins, their use poses serious security risks. This is because most units operate within the standard radio frequency range of 30MHz to 300MHz (VHF band), making it possible for a professional agent to intercept the conversation. Furthermore, a cordless telephone may respond to other units operating nearby, or to radio equipment, including citizen band (CB) type transceivers. Such interference could result in calls being dialled through a business's telephone unit(s) without the business's knowledge, possibly causing its calls to be misdialled.

Mobile car, marine and briefcase telephones are also susceptible to interception by an agent. Therefore, cordless and mobile systems are not recommended for use in any communication of business-related information of Grades 1 or 2, or for conversations of a confidential personal nature (see Classification of Information above).

Facsimile Machines

As a form of business communication, facsimiles have proven to be very effective in providing high-speed data transmission at very low costs. Their value as an integral part of a business's communication system is unquestioned. However, all users should recognize that the potential exists for documents to be inadvertently sent to an incorrect destination.

Such a breach could occur by misdialling the desired number or entering a totally incorrect number. Therefore, prior to transmission, it should be confirmed that the number is in fact, the correct one for the destination. Following this, the destination number should be entered into the facsimile machine with caution, then visually checked to make sure that the correct digits have been registered before executing the transmission command.

Two-Way Radio Systems

As with mobile and cordless telephone systems, two-way radio networks are highly susceptible to interception; even those employing some form of voice scrambler. They are, therefore, not recommended for communicating sensitive commercial information. There are, however, "secure" radio systems designed specifically to counter attempts at interception by any source of a threat up to and including Level 1. These systems are mainly used by the military, diplomatic missions of virtually all nations, but for any business that relies on two-way communication, such a secure system is a must. Manufacturers are usually listed in the "Yellow Pages" of most regional capitals.

Secure Communication Systems

Businesses which need to convey confidential information of a Grade 1 nature over the telephone network, a radio system, or via facsimile should consider installing an encryption unit to protect the data while it is being exchanged. These units offer an extremely high degree of security; the security is at a level which would surpass the requirements of even Grade 1 information. A professional agent attempting to intercept an exchange which is utilizing a cypher unit would only hear a stream of unintelligible chatter.

Encryption units can achieve this remarkably high degree of security by being able to randomly select from encryption codes which can be greater than 10 to the 30th power. If, for example, an agent was successful in intercepting and recording a scrambled message, he would need the services of a mainframe computer and perhaps months, or even years, of around-the-clock computing time in order to decipher the message. Facilities to do this are realistically only available to intelligence agencies of wealthy nations, and it would be a course of action not embarked upon unless the benefits outweighed the costs.

Document Storage

A business's first line of defence against penetration by a professional espionage agent is its external barriers, that is its doors and windows. Its second line of defense is the "containers" which house its confidential documents, for example, filing cabinets, index drawers, and microfiche vaults. It is therefore essential that businesses identify all documents and records that may be the target of a professional agent and secure these in containers which minimise the risk of their acquisition by unauthorized persons (also see the section on Classification of Information). The concern is with both the theft of the documents themselves and the undetected theft of the information they contain. So, to further reduce the risk of attack on containers designated for confidential documents, a business should not store valuables such as cash, securities, jewels, precious metals and narcotics in them.

Photocopying confidential documents or photographing them using a miniature camera loaded with high-speed film surreptitiously are the two most likely ways a professional agent could obtain documentary information without a business's knowledge. Another method, although very difficult to attempt, is to remove the document(s) from the business's offices, copy them and then return them to their storage container undetected. To guard against the former case, a locking device should be installed on the office photocopier strengthen this potentially weak security link. And to counteract both possibilities, businesses should always ensure that the containers housing their documents have locks and that the locks are used religiously. Metal containers, such as filing cabinets, with padlocks, offer a reasonably high level of security; however, safes and cabinets with combination locks incorporated as part of their physical structure offer a much higher level of protection.

Secure storage is equally applicable to computer disks and tapes and their "back-ups" (including off site storage of back-ups!). The control of keys for a business's document containers should follow those guidelines outlined previously.

Document Reproduction

The reproduction of classified documents bearing Grades 1, 2 and 3 should all be marked with the classification of the original material. Only sufficient copies necessary to meet operational requirements should be duplicated, and all reproductions should be destroyed as soon as they have served their purpose. Also, when photocopying sensitive documents always be cognizant of collecting the original(s) before leaving the machine.

Document Safeguards During Use

When confidential documents are not held in secure containers as outlined above, the person using the documents should:

(a) keep the documents under constant visual surveillance;

(b) place the documents in a storage container, cover it or turn it face down when an unauthorized person is present;

(c) return the documents to its designated storage container after use; and

(d) in the case blueprints, graphs, wall charts or other forms of visual aids, they should be labelled with a code name or code number and not openly bear a designation that could identify the project to an unauthorized observer.

Document Disposal

A business's wastepaper basket is an easily accessible source of information for the professional espionage agent. Probably two thirds of the paper generated by businesses and professional consultants contain information that is confidential to one degree or another, that is, information that if acquired by a competitor, could adversely affect business performance. This information gathering technique is known as a "trash cover" and is carried out simply by collecting the week's paper waste before the disposal truck arrives.

An easily overlooked source of information leakage is the photocopier. Spoiled and over-run copies should not be indiscriminately dropped into the wastepaper basket. An important acquisition for all businesses is a document shredder, and it is essential that it be used. Shredders, like locks, are of value only when they are put to work. There are several excellent units currently on the market, including compact models for the small business operator or professional consultant. An alternative for very large businesses is to use a bulk document destruction service. These companies are usually listed in the "Yellow Pages."

Another often overlooked source of information leakage is the impressions left on writing pads. To guard against this, a thin piece of aluminum, plastic or acrylic should be used under the top sheet of all memo pads and writing tablets to prevent the formation of impression marks. As with documents, all typewriter and printer ribbons, carbon paper, plates, stencils, drafts, stenographic notes, worksheets, and similar items should be destroyed—not just disposed of. Needless to say, that a readable copy can be obtained from any of these sources and therefore they are as dangerous as the originals in the hands of an adversary. Dictation recorded on tape or disks should be deleted immediately after being typed.

Microcomputers

Microcomputers pose specific security problems for businesses. The chief threats are from unauthorized hardware and software access, and software sabotage. In the main, the best countermeasures are those of sound physical and personnel security, and software management.

Countermeasures designed to protect computer software and data include:

1. Using passwords to authenticate legitimate users of the system;

    (a) Passwords should be impossible to guess, so it is advisable to avoid using any name that is common or familiar in the work environment, business, or to the project. Also, names that are significant to the user, for example, the wife/husband, child or pet's name should be avoided. Passwords consisting of six to eight letters or a combination of letters and numbers are ideal for a very high level of security.

    (b) Ensure that the software security program that controls user access does not display the password on the screen when logging on or appears on any print-outs.

    (c) Users should commit passwords to memory; they should never be posted on terminals, workstations or notice boards.

Above all, users should never tell anyone without proper authority a system's password.

(d) A system's password should not be changed at regular intervals, but randomly to foil any attempt to anticipate security changes.

2. Isolating information of various grades on separate disks and labelling each disk with its level of sensitivity, that is, Grades 1, 2, 3 or 4 as outlined in the section on Classification of Information.

3. Avoiding the use of fixed hard disks for storing sensitive data primarily because they cannot be readily removed for safe storage. A removable/portable hard disk offers a much higher level of security. If a fixed hard drive must be used for work associated with projects involving Grade 1 information, the alternative is to store the data on floppy disks.

4. Storing all disks (data disks, master program disks, and back-up program disks) in secure containers as outlined in the section on Document Storage.

5. Degaussing damage or defective disks which contain business information before returning them to the manufacturer or retailer for credit.

6. Degaussing disks before reuse for information of a lower Grade (see Classification of Information).

7. Disposing of printouts and printer ribbons as outlined in the section on Document Disposal.

8. Disposing of disks by shredding or degaussing, or both.

9. Shutting down idle terminals.

Countermeasures designed to protect computer hardware include:

1. Bolting the computer to the workstation (crude but very effective).

2. Locking the room when the system is not in use (effective in the case of protecting fixed hard disks).

3. Positioning computer screens to prevent viewing from windows, doorways or through glass partitions.

4. Allowing only trusted and qualified personnel to service or make modifications to a system.

5. Conducting electronic countermeasure sweeps at irregular intervals for bugs or wiretaps. Also, shielding cables leaving the computer room in conduit to prevent electromagnetic radiation which could be intercepted, and to deter illegal tapping (see sections on Electronic Surveillance and Telephone Wiring).

And countermeasures designed to guard against software sabotage include:

1. Using only commercial software from recognized, reputable software manufactures or custom designers.

2. Loading programs form the manufacture/designer's original copy.

3. Using only programs on an "approved programs list" in order to reduce the possibility of contracting program viruses, time-bombs and trojan horses from non-commercial software.

a) If non-commercial software must be used, for example, public-domain programs, shareware, freeware, and programs downloaded from bulletin boards, the software should first be thoroughly examined and tested for the possible presence of the sabotage mentioned in 3 above.

b) Before screening new, non-commercial, software products for viruses and the like, access to the system's hard disk should be temporarily blocked in order to avoid infection should there be any form of contamination in the program.

c) The examination of non-commercial software should include a text search to identify any suspicious signs of sabotage. That is, display all text strings in the program and look for messages like, "arf, arf, got you!," or other hints that the program may contain any form of time-bomb and trojan horse. The examination should also include multiple test runs utilizing all of the program's features, and the creation of several back-up copies of the program's contents (some viruses are known to be activated after being copied X times or being run for X hours, and still others have been programmed to unleash their havoc after a pre-set date/time).

d) Once new non-commercial software has passed rigorous screening, system users should then be supplied with approved (tested) copies of the program.

5. Implementing or upgrading back-up and recovery procedures which will facilitate a quick and complete reconstruction of a system's programs and data in the event that a saboteur strikes.

Finally, the security measures a business ultimately adapts to protect its micro-computer system should not be discussed with anyone outside of the organization. It is acceptable however, to acknowledge that measures to combat espionage and sabotage are in place, but the specific techniques and procedures should never be confirmed.

Video Display Units

The cathode ray tube of computer video display units is subject to what is commonly known as "burn-in." That is, data (images) can be etched into the phosphor on a unit's screen in the course of normal use. Therefore, VDUs should be inspected for evidence of burn-in by high intensity internal illumination prior to resale or transfer to other more "open" areas of a business's office environment, for example, reception areas.

Transmitting Sensitive Documents Through the Post

When a business needs to transmit documents of a Grade 1 or 2 sensitivity through the post, a service that is generically known as "registered mail" should be used. This service is designed to be the most secure method of posting articles of value. The postal service maintains a record on the article's whereabouts from lodgement to delivery, and for a small additional charge, a business can receive a receipt, signed by the addressee, confirming the document's delivery.

To prevent unauthorized viewing of the document's contents while in transit, it should be folded or packed so the text will not be in direct contact with the envelope or shipping container. Only substantially constructed, opaque envelopes, boxes and mailing tubes should be used for transmitting classified information. Although, another method is to enclose the documents in a shielding envelope, which in turn is placed in the addressed covering envelope. Care should be taken not to call unnecessary attention to the package by labelling it with a description of its contents. The outer envelope should be marked "DO NOT FORWARD. IF UNDELIVERABLE TO THE ADDRESSEE, RETURN TO SENDER." If the inner shielding envelope method is used, it should be annotated with "CONFIDENTIAL—TO BE OPENED BY THE ADDRESSEE ONLY."

Meetings and Conferences

If Grade 1 information is the subject of a meeting or conference the date, time, and location should only be promulgated to those people who will be attending, or on a need-to-know basis. Meeting organizers should be conscious of surveillance through windows and internal glass partitions. Agendas and conference notes should not be left behind but destroyed in the manner discussed under the section on Document Disposal. If the meeting breaks for refreshments, arrangements should be made to secure the room or have it kept under observation.

Reverse Engineering

Reverse engineering is another low-grade form of espionage, yet it has the potential to yield high-grade results. Essentially, reverse engineering is the purchase of a business's product (or service) and the subsequent disassembling of it into its component parts (or in the case of a service, a careful analysis of the service's quantity, quality, presentation, follow-up and so on) in order to determine how it was constructed and what manufacturing processes were utilized. Analysis of this type can provide an adversary with vital data about the targeted business. Such details can be likened to providing them with a guided tour of a business's facilities or "think tank." There may not be anything a business can do about this; however, every business should be cognizant that it will occur as soon as their product or service enters the market. Once a business begins its marketing phase, it will need to practice reverse engineering itself in order to ensure that competitors are not infringing patent rights (see Trademarks, Patents and Copyright). Although reverse engineering is an espionage technique, it is also an integral counterintelligence tool.

Trademarks, Patents and Copyright

Trademarks, patents, and copyright are all important elements in a business's counterintelligence effort. A trademark is any symbol, word, name or any combination of these that identifies a manufacturer's or merchant's goods (or services) and distinguishes them from those made or distributed by other businesses. Although there are common law rights granted to the user of a trademark, government registration provides prima-facie evidence that a business holds exclusive rights to its use, and to institute legal action against others for its unauthorized use. A trademark must be registered in each country in which a business trades. If this is not done, a foreign competitor could not only capitalize on a business's goodwill but wreak havoc by downgrading its product's reputation through less stringent business practices or quality control.

In contrast, a patent is a special right conferred on the designer of a unique process or device, enabling him to exercise exclusive privilege in its manufacture, use or sale for a limited period. A patent, like a trademark, must be applied for and is only enforceable in the country in which the registration is submitted. As with trademarks, if a business trades overseas, applications for the registration of a patent must be lodged with the appropriate government agency in each country in which trade is carried on. Again, if a business fails to do so a foreign adversary may seize its idea through its own intelligence efforts. If this happens, not only will the business have lost potential markets, it will have paid for all a competitor's research and development expenses.

Copyright, on the other hand, is a right that protects a broad range of intellectual material, from computer programs to works of art. Literature of all descriptions, musical scores, films, photographs and media broadcasts are also included under the copyright umbrella. Unlike trademarks and patents, copyright does not have to be applied for. Copyright protection is automatic, and copyright owners are protected in foreign countries under international convention. In order to afford full international protection to all intellectual property a business generates, a copyright notice should be placed in the fore of all published copies of the work. The copyright notice consists of the word *copyright* followed symbol © then the name of the copyright owner and the first year of publication.

Market Research

One of the aims of market research is to establish what need there is for goods and services by consumers. However, in some business circles market research is acknowledged to be a euphemistic title under which electronic and other forms of illegal espionage are conducted (see Chapter Two, the Espionage Function, and Chapter Three, Electronic Surveillance).

As discussed earlier in Chapter Three (Overt Sources of Information), there is an enormous number of open and semi-open sources of information which can supply a research analyst with raw data for conversation into finished, focused business strategies. This data may also be supplemented by information obtained by legal and acceptable covert operations, such as the time-honoured art of physical surveillance if need be. Given this, there really is no need to engage in illegal forms of information gathering. In fact, if it becomes known that a business uses such tactics, it will put its own attempts to thwart espionage by others at a great disadvantage. It could also lead to both severe criminal and civil penalties for all participants, including the body corporate and its directors.

In addition to playing an important part in making initial sales, market research plays a vital part in a business's counterintelligence effort, thus ensuring that the business continues to make sales (also see the section on Reverse Engineering). When used in this role, a business should closely monitor the information gathering process employed by research analysts. This will help ward off any possible illegal acts that may be perpetrated by over enthusiastic, naive, egotistical or careless researchers. Even though competitors may not exercise such restraint, curbing excessive zeal will put your business in a stronger position to deal with any external espionage threat.

Screening Personnel

The screening process for personnel should start at the application stage, with the applicant completing a detailed Personal History Statement (PHS). This should be carried out to prevent both the hiring of unethical people who may disclose confidential information and to frustrate any attempt at penetration by a professional agent (see the section on Infiltration this chapter). In addition to the applicant's full name, current residential and business address, and date and place of birth, the PHS can include such sub-histories as marital history, residential history, citizenship history, educational history, employment history, military history, criminal history and details like organizational memberships, and character, professional and credit references. (See Appendix B for an example of a Personal History Statement.)

When reviewing the applicant's PHS, any inconsistencies, discrepancies or unaccountable periods of two months or more should be verified. Even though an applicant may pass this initial screening process, once he is hired a probationary period should be set as a contingency for his possible dismissal should he be suspected of having become a security risk. Similarly, when an employee is promoted or assigned to sensitive duties, a screening procedure should ideally be conducted, covering the time elapsed from his initial hiring to the present. This is to ascertain if any factors in the promotee's recent past could jeopardize the confidentiality of the information he will be handling.

Another means of safeguarding sensitive information is by drawing up non-disclosure or secrecy agreements. These agreements are intended to create a psychological impression on employees, reinforcing the importance of protecting information to which they have been intrusted. These agreements are in effect, legal contracts and can be used as evidence in legal proceedings if an employee is found to be in violation of it (see Appendix C for an example of this type of agreement). Non-disclosure agreements should also be considered for temporary typing staff, contract cleaners, indoor plant gardeners and the like.

Recognising Physical Surveillance

Physical surveillance is the observation of people and places. There are many purposes for physical surveillance; some of these include obtaining information which may be difficult or impossible to obtain by any other method, to confirm information at hand, to develop "leads," and establish "links" between various people and between people and places. The information gleaned from such observations has inherent value. In addition, this raw information can be used to form the groundwork for more elaborate and extensive plans for information gathering.

All employees should be cognizant of the possibility of physical surveillance of their offices and themselves by a professional espionage agent. Being aware that something is out of place is an excellent way of recognising surveillance. It is, however, difficult to define "out of place." Persons loitering in halls, lobbies or stairways, suspicious visitors, frequent passers-by, and so forth should always be noted. If, after consideration, such activity is believed to be sufficiently suspicious, the Police should be notified. Employees should also be alert to possible surveillance from the street, adjacent buildings, parked motor vehicles and areas where employees park their cars.

Company vehicles themselves should be visually examined occasionally for any signs of "marking" by a professional agent. Identifying marks, such as broken tail light lens, removed light bulbs or pieces of reflective tape can assist an agent in distinguishing a vehicle in traffic and therefore aiding him in following its movements. Of higher sophistication and much less visible are mobile transmitters. These devices are usually attached to the underside of a car and can be located by careful visual inspection (see Appendix E for a list of various electronic surveillance devices).

Final Considerations

Confidential information should always be regarded as having a finite lifespan. It must be realized that despite the best engineered security plans and the installation of the most sophisticated counter-measures equipment, eventually information which is being guarded will become known to others. The American nuclear fighting capability became known to the world on the 6th of August 1945, the day before it was classified Top Secret.

Obviously, the best way to keep secrets is to store them in one's head and not communicate them to anyone. This is not a very realistic countermeasure in a business environment. The point to be made, however, is that as more people know about some particular secret, and the more that is written and recorded about it, the more likely that the secret will become prematurely known to unauthorized people (either inadvertently or by design). This was the case with American atomic bomb research; a Soviet espionage operation was able to penetrate the Top-Secret project and acquire that information well before the rest of the world even knew it existed. The second point to be made is once a professional agent knows or even believes that a business is guarding secrets, half of his work is already done; his next step is to devise a method to acquire it. The question every business must consider is, "how long is this information going to be secure"?

APPENDIX A
SAMPLE CHAIN OF CUSTODY RECORD

CHAIN OF CUSTODY RECORD

I, the undersigned, state that I took possession of the documents listed below on the date and time specified. Transfer of these documents was made as indicated. Further, that while in my possession, the documents were secure and inaccessible to unauthorized persons.

DOCUMENTS _____

CLASSIFICATION GRADE _____

1) INITIAL POSSESSION BY: _____

Time: _____

Date: _____

Signature: _____

2) TRANSFERRED TO: _____

Time: _____

Date: _____

Signature: _____

3) TRANSFERRED TO: _____

Time: _____

Date: _____

Signature: _____

4) TRANSFERRED TO: _____

Time: _____

Date: _____

Signature: _____

APPENDIX B
SAMPLE SECRECY DECLARATION

EXAMPLE ONLY

Your Business's Name
Address

DECLARATION OF SECRECY

I, _____

of _____

in the State of South Australia in the Commonwealth of Australia, do solemnly and sincerely declare, that, except in the course of my official duty with (NAME OF BUSINESS), I will not directly or indirectly communicate or divulge any information relating to any matter which comes to my knowledge as a consequence of my employment.

Signature: _____

Title: _____

Declared _____

this _____ day of _____19 _____

Before me: _____
Justice of the Peace

APPENDIX C
SAMPLE EMPLOYMENT
APPLICATION

APPLICATION FOR EMPLOYMENT
(NAME OF YOUR BUSINESS)

– STRICTLY CONFIDENTIAL –

Position applied for: ………………………………….

PERSONAL

1) Name: Last …………….. First ………… Middle …………

a) Previous name(s): …………………………………………..

2) Residential address: …………………………………………..

3) Home telephone: (   ) …………………………….

4) Date of birth: …………………………………………

5) Place of birth: …………………………………………

6) Marital status: …………………………………………

7) Drivers licence: Yes / No

  a) State: …………… b) Licence No.: …………..

  c) Licence type/class: ……………………………

8) If successful with this application, on what date would you be available to commence work: …………………………...

9) List the names, addresses and telephone numbers of two referees who are not related to you.

…………………………………………………………………

…………………………………………………………………

…………………………………………………………………

…………………………………………………………………

You may attach photocopies of your curriculum vitae, academic credentials, or any other supporting documents that you feel may be helpful in considering your application. Use additional pages if there is insufficient space to answer any of the following questions.

EMPLOYMENT HISTORY

10) Are you currently employed? ....

   a) Is it appropriate to contact your present employer for a work report? Yes / No

   b) Work telephone: (   ) ....

11) List your employment history, starting with current or last job and work back. Do not omit any period and include volunteer activities if applicable. A break in employment is to be explained. Please include the following details:

   a) Occupation

   b) Employer

   c) Employer's address

   d) Starting date

   e) Name of immediate supervisor

   f) Termination date

   g) Reason for leaving

12) In the last 5 years, have you ever been fired from a job? Yes / No

13) In the last 5 years have you ever resigned from a job after being notified that you would be fired? Yes / No

   If yes to either 12 or 13, please explain:

....

14) Have you ever been convicted of a felony? Yes / No

15) Have you ever been convicted of an offence involving violence? Yes / No

16) Are you currently on probation or parole? Yes / No

   If yes to 14, 15 or 16, please explain:

....

....

EDUCATION

17) List your educational history, including the following details:

   a) Name of school/college/university

....

   b) Years completed

....

   c) Certificate/Diploma/Degree awarded

....

   d) Description of course of study

....

   e) Specialized training, apprenticeship, skills, or

....

   other courses if applicable.

....

MILITARY SERVICE

18) Have you ever served on active duty in a branch of the armed forces? Yes / No If yes:

   a) which nation

....

   b) branch of service

....

   c) dates of active duty

....

d) rank held

....

e) type of discharge.

SPECIAL SKILLS AND QUALIFICATIONS

19) Summarize any special skills and/or qualifications you may have acquired through employment, study, or other experiences. Include membership to any organizations and any professional associations.

....

....

....

....

AGREEMENT

I certify that the answers given herein are true and complete to the best of my knowledge and belief and are made in good faith.

I authorize investigation of all matters contained in this application for employment as may be necessary for arriving at an employment decision, including a criminal record check with the relevant Police authority.

In the event of employment, I understand that false or misleading information given in my application, its attachments, or interview(s) may result in summary dismissal. I also understand that permanent appointment will be subject to an initial six-month probationary period

Signature of Applicant ....

Date ....

APPENDIX D
BOMB THREATS

If a bomb threat is ever received, it is important that the staff member receiving the call remain calm and composed. In the case of telephone threats, it is important to ascertain the validity of the threat as quickly as possible. Let the caller finish his message without interruption. Be sure to take down the message exactly as stated and note the time of its receipt. The staff member receiving the call should attempt to extract the following information from the caller, but keep responses short—two or three words at most:

a) when is the bomb set to go off;

b) what type of bomb is it;

c) where is the bomb located;

d) when was it placed;

e) why was it placed; and

f) who is calling, and how can they be reached.

If the building is occupied, clearly inform the caller that detonation may cause injury or death. If possible, the staff member should attempt to keep the caller on the line as long he can. As much information about the caller as possible should be learned to assist in identification. The type of information to be sought includes:

a) the caller's approximate age, sex and nationality;

b) the caller's accent—local, foreign etc.;

c) the caller's fluency—excellent, good, fair;

d) voice characteristics—loud, soft, deep, high pitched, intoxicated etc.;

e) speech—fast, slow, lisp, distinct, stutter, nasal etc.;

f) manner—clam, irrational, deliberate, emotional, coherent, angry etc.;

g) identifiable background noises—music, office machines, factory, street traffic, voices, quiet etc.;

h) name of group or person taking credit for the threaten bombing; and

i) whether additional threats/bombings can be expected.

It is essential for clam, careful listening, and exact reporting of the details.

If the threat is made by letter, carefully handle the letter, envelope, and anything it may contain, and preserve them by placing them in a NEW clear plastic bag. Police forensic experts may be able to analyze these for fingerprints, typewriting, handwriting and even the paper itself.

Any such threats should be reported immediately to the local Police authority and/or the Fire Service. It is suggested that the above check list be copied and placed in a convenient, but discreet, location by each office telephone for quick referral.

It is important to remember to never touch a suspected bomb. People should be moved away from the device; not the device moved away from the people (also see Covert Action Function in Chapter Two).

APPENDIX E
SUMMARY OF AUDIO
SURVEILLANCE DEVICES

MICROPHONES

DYNAMIC and CRYSTAL (general purpose)

No electric current required. Available in two directional patterns; omni- and cardio-.

CONDENSER (general purpose)

Battery powered. Generally, more sensitive than dynamic and crystal microphones. Usually available in only an omni-directional pattern.

TUBE MICROPHONES

Main feature is a hollow tube (miniature) fixed over a microphone element. Designed to be inserted through walls etc.

STETHOSCOPE MICROPHONES

Chief purpose—listening through solid objects (e.g., floors, ceilings, walls)

CONTACT MICROPHONES

Same as stethoscope microphones

SPIKE MICROPHONES

Same purpose as contact and stethoscope microphones, however, this device is distinguished by a spike shaped electronic "pick-up" (like a phonograph needle).

SHOTGUN/RIFLE MICROPHONES

A microphone which utilizes a cluster of varying length tubes to gain a directional pattern. Designed for eavesdropping across large, open areas.

PARABOLIC REFLECTORS

Similar in purpose to the shotgun/rifle microphone, however, the tubes are substituted for a parabolic collecting dish.

INDUCTION COILS

Not a microphone in the true sense. The device intercepts targeted audio signals via electrical induction. Chiefly used in telephone surveillance. Detection only by a physical search.

ANCILLARY DEVICES (general)

HIGH-GAIN AMPLIFIERS

Utilized to boost audio signals. Used commonly with contact, spike microphones, induction coils.

FREQUENCY EQUALIZERS

Used to eliminate background noise and other interfering sounds in electronic intercepts.

REMOTE CONTROL DEVICES

A transmitter/receiver combination, similar to those used by model hobbyists. It is used to switch surveillance equipment on and off from a distance.

VOICE OPERATED RELAY (VOX)

Used to start and stop tape recorders. Primary advantage is the conservation of tape, records only conversation, not periods of silence.

DROP-OUT-RELAY

Same purpose as a VOX, however, this device is used to turn a tape recorder on/off when it is connected to a telephone line. That is when the hand-set is removed from the hook the relay is tripped, starting the recorder; when replaced it turns the recorder off.

WIRELESS MICROPHONES (Miniature Transmitters)

VARIETIES

Numerous varieties exist from the most sophisticated to the very basic home-made or store shelf purchased.

RANGE

Transmission range depends on the sophistication of the unit's electronic circuitry, the placement of the transmitter (i.e.

interference caused by buildings, and steel structures etc. shorten range), and to some extent the sensitivity of the communications receiver.

POWER SUPPLY

Some devices use their own energy supplied via batteries. Others utilize the power of telephone lines or even the premises' AC power.

FREQUENCY

Commercially purchased and "home-made" transmitters are reported to operate around the commercial FM band, and adjacent to it; that is between 25 and 512 MHZ.

TRANSMITTER REPEATERS

A repeater is used in conjunction with a miniature transmitter which is installed in the target premise. The low power miniature transmitter broadcasts its signal to the secreted repeater. The repeater then boosts the signal strength and rebroadcasts the intercepted conversation on a different frequency.

HOMING TRANSMITTERS

These devices are fastened to, or secreted in, the target motor vehicle. The purpose is to declare the location of the vehicle to a surveillant who is tailing at a safe distance. They can emit either an audio tone or a series of beeps. Tracking is accomplished via radio direction finding/ signal strength devices. Locating the target vehicle can be enhanced by the employment of two tracking units to triangulate the transmitter's position.

LASER SURVEILLANCE

Primary purpose is to intercept audio communication. Operates by detecting the minute vibrations of a window caused by the room's internal audio. Consists of a laser, which projects a beam onto the target window, and a telescope/decoder, which detects the vibrations and translates them into sound waves (audio).

TELEPHONE DEVICES

DIRECT TAP

Acknowledged as the easiest method. Power is derived from the telephone line. Tap is affected by connection of headphones, tape recorder (VOX), or transmitter either in parallel or series. Parallel taps "load" the line and are easier to detect by an electronic counter-measure sweep, whereas a series tap does not.

NEAR DIRECT TAPS

These type of taps utilize induction coils. Devices can be configured to include headphones (live surveillance), tape recorder (VOX), or a miniature transmitter (and possible repeater).

BY-PASS WIRING

This operation involves the shorting out of the hook switch using either a resistor, capacitor, silicon-controlled rectifier, or a tone activated latching switch (infinity transmitter). Target instrument now acts as a hardwired microphone. Conversation can be monitored anywhere down the line. Cannot be used to monitor telephone conversation, only room audio with the handset on the hook.

ANCILLARY DEVICES (telephone)

CAPACITORS

Used to match the impedance of the surveillance device (e.g., headphones) to the telephone line, thus reducing the risk of a countermeasures sweep by indicating a 'load' on the line.

TRANSFORMERS

Same function as capacitors (e.g., tape recorders).

www.ingramcontent.com/pod-product-compliance
Lightning Source LLC
Chambersburg PA
CBHW022342280326
41934CB00006B/740